The Coming Avatar

Dorje Jinpa

Pentarba Publications

Also by Dorje Jinpa

The Book of Hermes

SENSA: The Language of the Sacred Mysteries

A Synthesis of Alchemy: An Inquiry into the Secrets of Hermetic
Philosophy

Essential Teachings of Maitreya: Three Complete Works

Secrets of the Heart: Awakening to Enlightenment

Knights of the Sacred Fire: An Introduction to the Agni Yoga
Teachings

Gates to Infinity: A Commentary on the Agni Yoga Infinity
Teachings

Available at pentarba.com

The Coming Avatar of Synthesis

> The Avatar about whom the scriptures speak is
> the Avatar of Synthesis. - Master Djwhal Khul

According to Master D.K. the 'Reappearance of the Christ,' the 'Externalization of the spiritual Hierarchy,' and the 'Coming of the Avatar of Synthesis,' is the **one** great world event for which all humanity waits. Much has been made public in the 'Bailey Books' concerning the reappearance of the Christ and the externalization of the Hierarchy, but of the "Heaven Silent One, Who stands behind and is the driving force for this event, little is known."

From the archives of the Hierarchy, translated by D.K. in his *A Treatise on Cosmic Fire*, we find the following prophesy concerning the Coming Avatar. [1]

* * * * * * *

From the gates of gold down to the pit of earth, out from the flaming fire down to the circle of gloom, rideth the secret Avatar, bearing the sword that pierceth.

Naught can arrest His approach, and none may say Him nay. To the darkness of our sphere He rideth alone, and on His approach is seen the uttermost disaster, and the chaos of that which seeketh to withstand.

---

[1] *A Treatise on Cosmic Fire*, Alice Bailey, page 747

The utmost disaster and chaos, which is already becoming evident, is caused in part by those resistant to the destined changes and from the fact that the keynote of the Coming Avatar is spiritual Will, Power, Synthesis, and that Divine Destruction that removes the old crystallized forms so that a New World may arise from the ashes.

* * * * * * *

The Asuras veil their faces, and the pit of maya reeleth to the foundations. The stars of the eternal Lhas vibrate to that sound, —the WORD uttered with sevenfold intensity.

The **Asuras**, who try to hide, are the 'Brothers of the Dark Face,' who have taken a stand against the spiritual evolution of the world. **The pit of maya** and **the circle of gloom** are symbols for the material world. **The stars of the eternal Lhas** are defined by H. P. Blavatsky as the 'spirits of the highest spheres.'[2] They have responded to the cries of Earth and the **WORD**, sounded forth by the Avatar **with seven fold intensity**.

* * * * * * *

Greater the chaos becometh; the major centre with all the seven circulating spheres rock with the echoes of disintegration. The fumes of utter blackness mount upwards in dissipation. The noise discordant of the warring elements greets the oncoming One, and deters Him not.

The strife and cries of the fourth great Hierarchy, blending with the softer note of the Builders of the fifth and sixth, meet His approach. Yet, He passeth on His way, sweeping the circle of the spheres, and sounding forth the WORD.

---

[2] See *Theosophical Glossary*, H. P. Blavatsky, page 188

The **fourth great Hierarchy** is the human kingdom. The **Builders of the fifth and sixth** are the two Angelic Hierarchies. The WORD that He sounds is the Vibration of his Silent Will, the Impulse of Synthesis—One Life, One Purpose, One Family!

"The constructive work of the Avatar of Synthesis," writes Master D.K., "will be apparent to you in the name He is known by; He is coming to the Earth in order to further the manifestation of unity, of oneness and of inter-relation, and He comes, therefore, to wield and apply first ray energy. He will charge or galvanize the three groups—the directing Agents in Shamballa, the Nirmanakayas, and the New Group of World Servers—with dynamic energy and in a mysterious way, relate them to each other so that a new synthesis and alignment will be present upon the Earth."[3]

The three groups to be energized by the coming Avatar are not the three main centres themselves, Humanity, Hierarchy, and Shamballa, but rather the three groups that act as *connecting links* between them. This, we are told, will dissolve the sharp dividing lines that separate them, bringing about, among other things, a closer unity between humanity and the Higher Worlds. The New Group of World Servers is made up of those goodwill activists in *all* fields of human endeavor, who work for the common good.

The Avatar of Synthesis, says Master D.K., is an extra-planetary avatar. "Bear in mind that those extra-planetary Avatars have not arrived at their high state of spiritual unfoldment on our planet or even in our solar system. Their origin, source, and spiritual relationships are a great mystery even to the Planetary Logoi — to whose help they go when the invocative appeal of any planet is adequate."[4] "These Avatars appear rarely but when they do, the effectiveness and results of their work are very great... They never

---

[3] *The Rays and the Initiations*, Alice Bailey, page 734
[4] *The Rays and the Initiations*, Page 734

descend lower than the mental plane… They bring about death—the death of the old and limiting forms and of that which houses evil."[5]

One of the primary functions of these extra-planetary avatars, says the Master, is to "Transfer egoic groups from one scheme to another," from one world to another.[6] This is suggestive, perhaps, of certain apocalyptic prophecies recorded in the New Testament. "Two shall be in the field, the one shall be taken, and the other left."[7] "In September 1940," says the Master D.K. "I spoke of Divine Embodiments as the highest type of Avatar for which humanity could look at this point in its evolution. I spoke of the activity of the Hierarchy and of Shamballa, should these two divine Agencies decide that intervention in the form of widespread cataclysm (engulfing all peoples) was necessary."[8] In 1945, at a time when the enemy's external threat through Hitler's armies had just been averted, the Master said that three recognitions must be evidenced by humanity before the year 2025, if the 'destruction of mankind is to be averted.'[9] They are:

1. Recognition of the Spirit of Christ within.[10]
2. Recognition of the Hierarchy of Masters that guide the evolution of the world.[11]
3. Recognition of the Way, the divine Plan.

---

[5] The Externalization of the Hierarchy. page 301

[6] A scheme is a great system of worlds. There are seven schemes in this solar system, each expressing a different space, time, and evolutionary development then the others.

[7] Matthew 24: 40

[8] Externalization of the Hierarchy, page 300. For more on the possibility of 'divine intervention through cataclysms' see *The Externalization of the Hierarchy*, page 259 & *The Rays and the Initiations*, page 555.

[9] *Discipleship in the New Age*, Vol. 2, Alice Bailey, page 164

[10] The divine spiritual essence within all living beings has been given other names: The Buddha Nature, The Atma, and Christos, to name a few.

[11] While the existence of the Hierarchy has nearly always been a closely guarded secret a few names have found according to the prevailing culture. The Great White Brotherhood, Bodhisattvas, Masters of Wisdom, Rishis, Children of the Sun, Daemons, Cloud of Witnesses, Celestial Heros, Brothers of Humanity, The Hierarchy of Watchers, Sons of Resurrection, Guardians of Light, Dragons of Wisdom, and Immortals.

The destruction mentioned here could mean something like the great flood of the last days of Atlantis, although the Master points out that some prophecies say that destruction by fire is also a possibility. "If humanity fails to unite under the banner of the Forces of Light against the forces of material aggression and selfishness, then the 'fiery ordeal' might be unavoidable."[12]

In 1940 Master D.K. announced that: "Another and lesser Avatar is also waiting a call from humanity. He is esoterically related to the Avatar of Synthesis, being overshadowed by Him. This Avatar can descend on to the physical plane into outer expression and can thus step down and transmit the stimulation and quality of the force of the greater Avatar Who can come no nearer than the mental plane. Who this Coming One may be is not yet revealed. It may be the Christ, if His other work permits; it may be the One chosen by Him to issue forth, overshadowed by the Avatar of Synthesis and directed in His activities by the Christ, the Lord of Love."

A few years later the Master announced that the Avatar of Synthesis would overshadow the Christ, the Manu, and Master Morya, thus creating "a triangle of energies into which (and through which) the energy of the Avatar of Synthesis can pour, finding right direction under Their combined efforts."

The Christ "will come again as the World Savior, but owing to the stupendous nature of the work ahead, He will be fortified and buttressed by the 'Silent Avatar' Who (occultly speaking) will 'keep His eye upon Him, His hand beneath, and His heart in unison with His."[13]

In all the religious and esoteric scriptures concerning the coming Avatar—Buddhist, Hindu, Persian, Christian, and those of the Ancient Mysteries—He is depicted as riding a white horse, thus symbolizing the overshadowing of the lesser Avatar by the greater.

---

[12] *The Externalization of the Hierarchy*, page 259
[13] *The Rays and the Initiations*, page 94-95.

Master D.K. hints at this when speaking of the lesser Avatar and the 'Rider on the White Horse,' he says, "in an earlier cycle, the then initiates spoke of the 'sacrificial horse.'[14] In Hindu scriptures the next incarnation of Vishnu, as avatar and world savior, will be as Kalki, whose name means the white horse. According to certain Tibetan myths relating to the coming Avatar, the Horse on which He rides is an incarnation of a great Bodhisattva. Edgar Cayce, in his highly veiled commentary on the *Book of Revelation*, states that the horse ridden by the White Horse Rider, is the Christ.[15]

According to the Agni Yoga Teaching the Kali-Yuga, the age of darkness and ignorance, is now coming to an end, and the forces of darkness are therefore fighting hard to resist the incoming light of the new Satya Yuga, the age of truth and light. "Anyone who knows about the approaching end of the Kali Yuga understands that it cannot occur without world upheavals. The forces that were particularly powerful during the 'Black Age' must now struggle for survival. They prefer a general catastrophe to defeat."[16]

In the Matsya Purana,[17] an ancient Hindu scripture, Master Morya is called Maru, also spelled Moru, a great Sage of the Maurya lineage, who is said to be still living in the Himalayan Mountains, and who will come forth at the beginning of the Krita Yuga. Krita Yuga is another name for the Satya Yuga, the Age of Truth.[18]

The Kalachakra Tantra, given by the Buddha, states that the Avatar Rigden Dragpo or Jyepo, also known Kalki Rudracakrin, will, at the end of the Dark Age (Kali Yuga) ride forth on a white horse

---

[14] *Externalization of the Hierarchy*, page 304
[15] *The Revelation: A Commentary Based upon a Study of Twenty-Four Psychic Discourses.* Page 135. This esoteric commentary veils hidden spiritual events through their correspondences to the centers of the body.
[16] *Supermundane 127*
[17] (chapter ccixxii)
[18] Also see *The Secret Doctrine* by H. P. Blavatsky, Adyar Edition, Vol. 2., Page 93.

(in some accounts blue) from Shamballa to destroy the evil in the world.[19]

The Bhagavata Purana says: "Lord Kalki will appear to the king of Shamballa. He will be mounted upon his swift horse, Devadatta. He comes with his sword to destroy the evil kings of the world." Devadatta means 'a gift of the gods.' "Maru [Morya] and Devapi, possessing great yogic powers, will descend from Shamballa with Kalki, the Avatar." [20] Edwin Bernbaum in his book *The Way to Shamballa* writes: "In the *Kalki Purana*, a sage King named Maru [Morya], a descendant of an earlier incarnation of Vishnu, lives there in the Himalayas, awaiting the end of the age of discord [Kali Yuga]. When Kalki comes to liberate the world, this sage will join him in the final battle against the barbarians. After their victory over the forces of evil, Maru will gain a throne and assist Kalki in establishing a golden age." [21] A similar prophecy can be found in the *Vishnu Purâna* (Book IV, Chapter 4) where it is stated that there was in the Sorya Dynasty a king called "Maru, who, through the power of yoga, is still living in the village called Kalapa," in the Himalayas and who "in a future age, will be the restorer of the Kshatriya race in the solar dynasty." The Kshatriyas is a race Warrior Kings. Kalapa is considered to be on the northerner side of the Himalayas.[22]

---

[19] *The Way to Shamballa*, by Edwin Bernbaum, pages 172, 177-178.

[20] XII, 2.

[21] Pages 83-84.

[22] See H.P. Blavatsky Collected Writings Vol. VI, page 40-41

The above print is a detail from a painting magically precipitated by Master D.K. for H.P. Blavatsky at her request showing Morya at His home in the Himalayas. It is signed Gai Ben-Jamin, a name by which Master D.K. was known in the early days of the Theosophical Society. The original precipitation on silk is housed at the Theosophical Headquarters at Adyar.

"The energy coming from the Avatar of Synthesis," say Master D.K., "will make its primary impact upon this [Morya's] Ashram, which provides the line of least resistance."[23]

St. John also prophesied the coming of the Avatar in his *Book of Revelations*:

> I saw the heavens open and behold a white horse; and He that sat upon him is He who makes faith and knowledge true, and in righteousness he doth judge and make war. His eyes were as a flame of fire, and on His head were many crowns; and He had a name written, that no man knew, but He Himself. And He was clothed in vesture dipped in blood: and his name is

---

[23] Externalization of the Hierarchy, page 662

called the WORD of God. And out of mouth goeth a sharp sword, that with it He should smite the nations: and He shall rule them with a rod of iron: and He treadeth the winepress with the fierceness and wrath of almighty God. And he hath on His vesture and on His thigh a name written, 'King of Kings, and Lord of Lords.'[24]

Paul Davidson, in his little know *Book of Light and Life or the Essence of the Sohar*, writes of the obvious similarity between the Hindu Kalki Avatar who comes riding a white horse to conquer the forces of evil and the Rider on the white horse of the Book of Revelation. He also refers to a similar prophecy from the *Zend Avesta*. "The White Horse upon which Sociosh [the Mazdean saviour][25] rides, like Vishnu, is the 'Horse of the Sun,' Shiloh is the Sun's city, and Sociosh is the God-Messiah, or King coming from the Sun... The Arabs represented Iauk (Iach) by a Horse, the Horse of the Sun."[26] (The Kalachakra also speaks in an esoteric manner of the seven

[24] 19: 11-16
[25] See *The Theosophical Glossary* by H.P. Blavatsky, page 306 Also spelled 'Sosiosh' & 'Saoshyant.'
[26] 1891, page 53

horses of the sun.) According to H.P. Blavatsky, "Sosiosh is the prototype of 'the faithful and the true' of the *Revelation*, and the same as Vishnu in the *Kalki-Avatara*. Both are expected to appear as the *Saviour of the World, seated on a white horse* and followed by a host of spirits or genii, mounted likewise on milk-white steeds." This could means that the overshadowed Lesser Avatars, in their turn, overshadow certain initiates of their ashrams. Master D. K. states that this may indeed be the case. We might note here that Master Morya is also depicted riding a white horse.

The Root Kalachakra Tantra states: "Kalki Rudra, possessed of the Great Wheel, who by skillful speech and the best horse samadhi, will put an end to the barbarian dharma." 'The best horse samadhi,' may be an esoteric reference to the technique of 'overshadowing' through the power of yogic meditation. The 'great wheel' is often depicted in paintings of the Avatar.

In that great wordless picture book of the ancient Mysteries, *The Book of Hermes,* the thirteenth hieroglyph depicts much the same symbolism.

Note that the Rider is greeted by the Hierophant, the one who confers initiation into the sacred Mysteries, and that the 'city of Light,' reminiscent of the 'New Jerusalem,' lies in the forward distance or future. The death and destruction implied here pertains to that which is obstructing the Way, the natural evolutionary flow.

According to Master D. K. the Avatar is needed at this time because "the separateness of humanity, and its selfishness, had reached such vast proportions and its effects were so completely dominated by the forces of evil, that—in response to the massed inchoate demand of humanity—the Hierarchy called for spiritual interposition. The endless selfish propaganda, in speech or in writing, most of it materialistic, nationalistic and basically untrue and wrongly motivated, became such a clamor that it reached to spheres usually impervious to the sounds of earth; the Avatar of Synthesis was called in to aid."[27] A very ancient Hindu prophecy from the *Vishnu Purana* states that before the 'Formless One' will appear, "Wealth will be decreasing day by day until nearly the whole world will be deprived.

---

[27] The Externalization of the Hierarchy, page 648

Property alone will confer rank. Devotion will be given to wealth alone. Passion will be the sole bond between the sexes. Falsehood will be the only successful means of litigation. Women will be merely objects of sensual gratification. The Earth will be venerated only for its mineral treasures."

When is the Silent Avatar coming? According to both the Hindu and the Buddhist scriptures[28] the Avatar will come at the end of the Kali Yuga, the present age of darkness. Some will argue that according to Hindu scriptures the end of the Kali Yuga will not take place for hundreds of thousands of years. But we must remember that the Wheel of Time, upon which the yugas are based are of two kinds—greater and lesser. The Kali Yuga of the lesser cycle the now coming to an end. The greater cycle, which corresponds to what the Theosophists call the 'Fourth Round' (the lowest), will continue for a long time. The author of the Agni Yoga Books, reverently called the 'Teacher,' says that we are now at the end of the Kali Yuga, though he also states that this depends to some degree upon humanity. And in his book *Agni Yoga* 307 we read, "The East knows of the Army of Fiery Warriors that will arise before the coming of the New Era." These warriors are also known as the Knights of the Sacred Fire. H.P. Blavatsky also states that we are nearing the end of the Kali Yuga, the Dark Age. Khedrup Norsang Gyatso (1423-1513), a disciple of the 1st Dalai Lama calculates, from the hints given in the *Kalachakra Tantra,* that Kalki Rudracakrin will conquer the barbarians in the year 2424.[29] In June of 1943 Master D.K. wrote; "Ask me not for the date or the hour, brother of mine, for I know it not." But "you will know when the Avatar links up with the planetary Logos because I will then give you the final Stanza of the Great

---

[28] *Kalki Purana, The Vishnu Purana,* and *The Kalachakra Tantra.*
[29] *Ornament of Stainless Light: An Exposition of the Kalacakra Tantra.* Wisdom Publications, page 614.

Invocation."[30] This He did in April of 1945. This 'link' between the Avatar and the Logos marked the first step to His manifestation that will continue through the reappearance of the Christ and the externalization of the Hierarchy, which is still to come. The externalization of the Hierarchy, says the Master, could begin as early as 2025.

According to the *Vishnu Purana* the Kalki Avatar will "re-establish righteousness upon earth. The minds of those who live at the end of age of strife [Kali Yuga] shall be awakened and shall become translucent like crystal. The humans who are thus changed by virtue of that peculiar time shall become the seeds of a new race, who shall follow the laws of the golden age of purity."

* * * * * * *

From the nadir to the zenith, from the eve unto the day be with us, from the circle of manifestation to the center of pralayic peace, is seen the enveloping blue, lost in the flame of achievement.

This verse depicts the rise of the Avatar along with those He has liberated from the circle of gloom. **From the nadir** (a point above the observer that is also the lowest point that the Avatar descends), **to the zenith** (the highest point above the observer). **From the eve** (the Age of Darkness), **to the day be with us** (the Age of Truth). **From the circle of manifestation** (the physical plane), **to the center of pralayic peace, is seen the enveloping blue lost in the flame of achievement.** Pralaya is the abstraction from time and space and form and absorption into Pure Spirit. For a human being this is called nirvana. The **center of all enveloping blue** is the Auric Egg,

---

[30] The Rays and the Initiations, pages 93 & 95. The 'final Stanza' pertains to the Great Invocation its present well-known form.

sometimes called the Body of Light. The world of form and separation is lost from sight in the achievement of divine union.

What can we do to prepare for this unprecedented event? The Master D.K. gives four suggestions:

"1. The effort to stand with all other disciples and aspirants in an attempt to call forth the Avatar, to reach Him by focused intensive thought and to evoke His response. This is the purpose of the new Invocation.

2. Providing a nucleus or group through which the Avatar of Synthesis can work when the lesser Avatar has come forth upon the physical plane....

3. Constructing a network of light and service in every land....

4. Preparing the general public for the Coming One..."[31]

And how long will the Formless One remain? Master D.K. says that the triangle of energies through which the Avatar of Synthesis is to manifest with the Christ at the center, "will continue for two thousand five hundred years,"[32] or till the end of the Aquarian Age.

Another ancient prophecy preserved in the archives of the Hierarchy and translated by Master D.K.:

'The Sons of men who are now the Sons of God will withdraw their faces from the shining light and radiate that light upon the sons of men who know not yet they are the Sons of God. Then shall the Coming One [the lesser Avatar] appear, His footsteps hastened through the valley of the shadow by the One of awful power [the Avatar of Synthesis] Who stands upon the mountain top [the highest point of the mental plane], breathing out love eternal, light supernal, and peaceful silent Will. Then will the sons of men respond. Then will a newer light shine forth into the dismal weary vale of earth. Then will new life course through the veins of men, and

---

[31] Externalization of the Hierarchy, pages 311-312.
[32] The Reappearance of the Christ. Page 98

then will their vision compass all the ways of what may be. So peace will come again on earth, but a peace unlike aught known before. Then will the will-to-good flower forth as understanding and understanding blossom as goodwill in men."[33]

* * * * * * *

Up from the pit of maya back to the portals of gold, forth from the gloom and darkness back to the splendour of day, rideth the Manifested One, the Avatar, bearing the shattered Cross.

Naught can arrest His return, none can impede His Path, for He passeth along the upper way, bearing His people with Him. Cometh the dissolution of pain, cometh the end of strife, cometh the merging of the spheres and blending of the hierarchies. All then is re-absorbed within the orb, the circle of manifestation. The forms that exist in maya, and the flame that devoureth all, are generated by the One Who rideth the Heavens and entereth into the timeless Aeon.[34]

The passage, **He passeth along upper way, bearing His people with Him**, might be illuminated somewhat by another prophecy given by Master D.K.

I may point out (even though it is not possible to give more than a hint) that the force of the Cosmic Transferer [one of the names of the Avatar] is being called into activity by the

---

[33] Isid page 95
[34] *A Treatise on Cosmic Fire* page 748

transference during this cycle [of 2500 years] of a special group of highly advanced units of the human and deva kingdoms (members of the occult Hierarchy) to another scheme altogether.[35]

This great Event, the coming Avatar of Synthesis, and the descent of the Christ and His Hierarchy to the Earth, also includes the restoration of the Mystery Schools, the cosmic initiation of Sanat Kumara (the Lord of the World), and the transformation of our sphere into a Sacred Planet.

"It will be obvious," says Master D. K., "if you have considered my words carefully, that a great spiritual movement is under way— *perhaps the greatest of all time!*"[36]

* * * * * * *

From the far reaches of Space
May the Avatar of Synthesis come forth.
Come forth Oh Mighty One!
Aum Svaha!

---

[35] *A Treatise on Cosmic Fire*, page 446
[36] *Externalization of the Hierarchy*, page 649.